Dancing through Fire

Daily Poems of Wisdom, Passion, and Peace

TINA DATSKO DE SÁNCHEZ

Foreword by Elena Larssen

Open Waters Publishing
an imprint of The Pilgrim Press
1300 East 9th Street,
Cleveland, Ohio 44114
thepilgrimpress.com

Published 2023.

Printed on acid-free paper.

Library of Congress Cataloging-in-Publication Data on file.
LCCN: 2021943799

ISBN (paper) 978-0-8298-1223-7

Printed in The United States of America.

Original cover artwork by Loryn Spangler-Jones
Book and cover design by Meredith Pangrace

For my parents, Joseph and Doris Datsko,
whose belief in me gave me the courage
to believe in myself.

CONTENTS

20. I believe Love will prevail and the lovers,
21. What I am here for it seems is nothing
22. Clouds nest on the mountain's shoulders
23. A foggy August morning, a chill
24. Late in August, the pomegranate puts forth
25. The five points of the maple leaves
26. Soup warming my stomach, Vivaldi swirling the air,
27. Connection is the essence of life:
28. Over a holiday meal our neighbor tells us
29. In wisdom is balance, harmony, moderation.
30. Tonight in the meditation circle, kneeling down,

Thirty Poems of Passion

1. Diving in is the essential act.
2. Hearing the majesty of Purcell's "Trumpet Voluntary"
3. On the flight back from Michigan,
4. The passion of grief is like a river,
5. Where is the passion in grief?
6. Orange roses float among white orchids;
7. Walking down the red carpet, I see how small
8. The violet-speckled orchid sends out lush blooms
9. This first spring day of sitting outdoors on the patio
10. What lies beneath this fear of earthquakes?
11. Heat and languor pour down upon me.

12. Neither glowing skin, nor veins and muscles beneath,
13. The piano that thundered above her childish head
14. Grief's passion surges through lungs and fingertips;
15. Let us recall the point of the passion stories—
16. At the heart of our meditation circle,
17. It is hunger for God that lights the flame.
18. Take off the glasses of perceiving dualities
19. Pink and yellow roses bloom again in my garden.
20. There was once a whale who thought to live
21. The pomegranate tree puts forth its first two buds.
22. Passion's fire cleanses me.
23. Today I know that each person's death
24. Pain can be a purifier.
25. The way to pull the plug on pain is forgiveness:
26. Sometimes it takes a breaking of our hard
27. When passion becomes compassion
28. When that old invisible ghost starts shaking the table,
29. The buzzing saw next door cuts through my contemplation
30. The nature of pain, just as the nature of grief,

Thirty Poems of Peace

1. What do you think peace is anyway?
2. Write all your worries in a letter to God
3. Peace is not an only child. She is a middle child,

4. Let me pour words into you like rain on parched earth.
5. Dear ones, let go all your striving, let go
6. Standing still as a tree planted in the garden,
7. A balloon filled with warm air from an ardent fire
8. Under a mostly clouded sky,
9. God calls us to find new lovers.
10. God, split me wide like ripe fruit.
11. In this morning's rain the world grows silent
12. Ease now flows like honey, sweet and golden.
13. Like an adoring dog awaiting your return,
14. Why does the moon shine less brightly than the sun?
15. In Zumba class we jump from side to side
16. A bit of motion caught from the corner of my eye:
17. What can I tell you about peace?
18. We are each a piece of the peace.
19. Life's precious dance is dancing in me.
20. Peace is found in the stillness.
21. The journey from pain to peace
22. This Advent season I now comprehend:
23. Hunting for God is a skill the wise develop.
24. Ease is a golden balm that fills us if we let it.
25. Lean in closely and I will whisper to you:
26. Sitting on the patio eating a pomegranate
27. A grain of sand that thinks it's alone

FOREWORD

Spirituality is multifaceted.

Spirituality keeps defying definition.

Spirituality can call to mind knees folded in prayer or arms stretched in salutation to the sun. Spirituality may mean singing from a pew or choir loft, or the gentle counting of breath. Spirituality may be personal and solitary, or deeply communal, meditation or exultation. Seen one way, there are traditions and practices. Seen another, there are experiences and intensity. For one, spirituality might mean reaching into ancient books. For someone else, it might be letting go of images and ideas and leaning into pure experience.

In a complicated and multifaceted world, finding the words to express our spirituality is a challenge. The classic definition of spirituality as the journey to orient oneself to God has grown. Today, it includes exploring one's values and apprehending the sacred in many forms. Spirituality in a fast-paced world may mean pausing to acknowledge the present moment and acknowledging that which is greater than the moment. When religion stalls out in correct behavior and right speech, spirituality lures us to recall the integrity of experience.

For Tina Datsko de Sánchez, spirituality is both public and private, ancient and modern. Her spirituality is both about the words and the space between the words, where breath and motion and dance can occur. When you read one of Tina's poems, you pick up a multifaceted object and see light bounce in different colors, different directions. You might see something you've never seen before.

Tina and I had the joy of a pastor-parishioner collaboration during my years as Senior Minister of the First Congregational Church of Long Beach, United Church of Christ. This congregation has been persistently progressive in its theology, worship, and witness since 1888. On the Pacific Rim of North American, that date makes the congregation one of the oldest continuously operating institutions in Los Angeles County, even older than the Long Beach fire department. And yet, throughout that history, the question of spirituality was democratized and full of respectful curiosity. The same conventional prayers and spiritual cliches would never quench the thirst of this inventive and intellectual church!

Fortunately, we had Tina. We would meet with our creative Worship and Arts Ministry Team and pore over the seasons of the church: Advent and Christmas, Lent and Easter, the annual fall season when Ordinary Time became a practice and celebration of community and ecclesiology. We were a group that loved the tradition but couldn't rest until it was reviewed, reinterpreted, and recast for a contemporary and diverse congregation. We loved a good theme, a new image. If it didn't connect the Spirit with the pursuit of social justice, it didn't pass muster. For us, Tina wrote poetry, prayers, lyrics for Christmas Cantatas, reader's theatre, litanies, and helped us write new verses to add to classic hymns.

When Tina cast theological reflection into poetry two things happened: correctness and "saying it all right" melted away and left space for the Spirit to enter, between the lines of a gem-like poem. Then, our yearning for transcendence became language.

Spirituality as we know it will change. Religion may or may not hold its vitality. But the words and the space between the words may make all the difference.

Peace,
The Rev. Elena Larssen

PREFACE

After completing the ninety poems that make up *Swimming in God*, the muse continued to show up, and the poetry kept pouring through me. I made it a custom to show up and listen at least once a week, usually on Mondays, to get my energy going for the week. This became a spiritual practice focused on paying attention and listening deeply. Feeling centered and connected to the divine loving energy of the universe brought bliss. Focusing on a theme for thirty poems allowed me to explore different facets and experience that issue across the flow of time. The process felt like writing one poem in many parts that developed variations on the theme.

I am convinced this poetry blossomed as a result of my being deeply rooted in a supportive community. During this period, I continued participating in the bi-weekly meditation group called Sacred Practices at the First Congregational Church of Long Beach. I began to co-lead with Dr. Robert Kalayjian, who is also a trained instructor in Mindfulness-Based Stress Reduction. Some of the poems reflect the exquisite moments of our practice together. In the safe space of this group, I started sharing some of the poems to give them a test drive. Group members told me that they resonated with the poems. This allowed me to see that the poems could contribute usefully to individuals exploring their own spiritual journeys.

Much as with the poetry in *Swimming in God*, many of the poems in this second book of the series were born out of experiences of grief and loss. In September 2008, I began writing "Thirty Poems of Wisdom" following the experience of recuperating from a collapsed lung. In February 2010, "Thirty Poems of Passion" began showing up, a few days before my mother died suddenly from a heart attack on Valentine's Day. Grieving the loss of my mother colored that group of poems, which explore passion in its connotations of pain and suffering. From September through December 2010, I began writing my way toward peace with "Thirty Poems of Peace."

Throughout these challenges Rumi and Hafiz continued to be my companions on the path. I kept up the practice of reading their poetry daily. I was learning from them a different form of poetic encounter—one based on playfulness and surprise. They showed me how to let a poem twist or suddenly expand into new layers of meaning. Immersed in their songs, I also began to imbibe some of the flavor of Sufi poetry. Some of the favorite metaphors for spiritual experience included spirit as wine, the spiritual meeting place as a tavern, and God as the tavern keeper. The true seekers were presented as being more at ease with the rough customers of the tavern than with pious folk. Above all, Rumi and Hafiz coached me to move beyond poetic conventions I had internalized from poetry workshops in college and graduate school. It is with gratitude for this teaching that I offer the following poem.

AT LAST I HAVE FOUND FRIENDS

As a poet who doesn't want to nail words
to the page but get them up and dancing—
words that get drunk with abandon
and go carousing 'til dawn.
Words that refuse to toe the line
and laugh at bandied terms like responsibility.

Words that love to sing, and more than anything
love to kiss. Words that sneak up on you,
and plant a big wet smackeroo on your lips.
Unruly, wayward words that praise ecstasy not dogma.

How does a poet with a gang of words
like that find friends?
Not among the pursed lips and puckered brows
of ivory towers or bastioned journals.
Such a poet gets more respect
from courtesans and thieves.

So at last I have found friends.
Hafiz and Rumi are like two rascally
elder brothers who would take their gypsy
sister out to the wildest tavern
where golden wine will spill all over the floor.
In no time she'll be up on the table dancing,
because her brothers have taught her well.

Desire is only a precursor to thirst—
for when thirst burns and aches
with a stitch in the side from dancing
and dancing, then the vintner himself
will come out aproned and pour the next round.

—Tina Datsko de Sánchez

"…each life crisis can become a crucible for
both a psychological and a spiritual rebirth."
—Michael Meade, "Paths of Initiation"

Thirty Poems of Wisdom

1.

What is the best thing I can say to you today?
Love is everywhere: palpable in the air we breathe,

in light entering our eyes, in vibrations of music,
the fragrance of lilies, the taste of an apple.

Love assaults us on every front, every sense.
How can we help but shout and dance our gratitude?

2.

Look around you! The hibiscus grow with such
fierceness and determination. They know
no discouragement. Cut them back

and soon green shoots become new branches
and joyous luscious blooms. There's no telling them,
"It's not worth the bother, just give up."

How did they get so wise?
By eating and drinking light.

3.

The spider strings its web between two palms.
Wishing it gone only comes from fear.
Why see it as creepy and predatory?

It weaves its tapestry all day and hangs
there, filling up with light, to glow orange at dusk.
Do I not do the same, as best I can?

4.

God, how do you look on my drunkenness?
I long for you and nothing else matters.

My day wears thin, except when I speak
of you, when I touch you singing.

Am I hopelessly out of control?
Or am I the foot of the dervish

centered and grounded to earth
like a temple pillar around which Rumi whirled?

5.

The gold flecks on Rumi's book jacket
rub off and sparkle on my palms.

Just so, dear friend, your passion rubs off
and sparkles in my whole being.

This thirst for the beyond, and way beyond
all things, the wow!

And then the sparkles illuminate all things—
palm tree, hibiscus, day lily, rosebud—

all made achingly real by the
sacredness of their unreality.

6.

Desire burns in me as though
even my clothing would ignite and flame.

I am a torch that only lives
to metabolize life into light.

I hunger so for the real, the intangible divine—
my soul thirsts for its lover's kiss,

for a togetherness where all separateness ends
and pure flowing being begins.

Surely God has created us for this.

7.

Nothing and everything lies within.
A wellspring exists to flood the inner landscape.
Uncap it and play, like children play

in an open fire hydrant in July.
Water bursts upward and pours downward.
This rain drenches deeper than skin

and quenches the eternal thirst of living.
You are your own fountain.
No one else can open the way for you.

8.

The tenderness of lovemaking and
the fierceness of lovemaking—
all is in the Beloved.

God breaks us open to expose every wound,
then covers each one with sacred kisses
and massages in a healing balm.

Surrender to the loving physician within.

9.

Wisdom is balance—a half-moon pose,
arms and legs stretch in opposing directions,
yearning for God.

And the center reckons stillness and balance.
With love as a wheel or a web, we cast
our nets wide and float, supported.

10.

You are not what you take in.
You are like grape juice that can turn to wine.

The mystical ingredient turns the harsh
to gentle and the bitter to sweet.

Alone, in the quiet of the bottle, Spirit appears
and manufactures the many actions that are love.

11.

A swollen joint or injured limb:
is it really a curse, a punishment?
Or a signal that one is ready to be healed?

In healing and growth, the Divine shines forth.
There is beauty in this also. Could this be
why we delight so in budding leaves and flowers?

12.

Last fall our neighbor pruned
our pomegranate tree, teaching it
to bear fruit by focusing its energies.

This spring the pomegranate's leaves
burst forth with even greater
joy in fewer places.

13.

Our friend Ed said it best:
"Happiness is found at the intersection
of pleasure and meaning."

Does it matter then whether one walks
the road of pleasure, stopping at meaning's crossings
or the road of meaning, stopping at pleasure?

14.

Truly seeing is believing. Look there
at sunlight illuminating new pomegranate leaves,

their red tips glowing with possibility
and even certainty: spring is coming.

That light is God's caress, God's laughter,
God's invitation to join the riotous song and dance.

15.

Be the welcome you wish to receive.
Let radical acceptance wash through you

like a flash flood. Greet all beings
who show themselves to you inside or outside

with honor and love. God's arms are wide
enough to embrace all. Be those arms embracing.

16.

This morning practicing tai chi,
relaxing and moving and relaxing more,

I sense the atoms of this body interpenetrating
with atomic particles of air, house, garden, light.

In a sense, I do not exist, while existing
at one with waves in motion all around.

17.

Easter day at a friend's memorial:
remembrance of death contains a resurrection.

Awaken to the eternal. Let the hammer strikes
of hours crucify the sleepwalked life,

and rouse us to the now-ness, the unique
irretrievable beauty, of this shimmering moment.

18.

You speak through poets
and dance through dancers.

You cook through chefs
and love through lovers.

In all that moves and sings,
you are moving and singing.

19.

Trust who you are, because what flows in you
is not you. Rely on the Beloved
who is bigger than your fears.

Strive to be as big as Love.
That great wind, bigger than a hurricane,
spins the universe with songs of joy.

20.

I believe Love will prevail and the lovers,
transformed, will weave their lives together

as dancers weave space together,
awakening it to itself and God within it.

I do not claim to be psychic, though spending my days
as poets do—with one ear pressed to the heart of the universe.

21.

What I am here for it seems is nothing
but love, nothing more and nothing less.

Love stretches my skin daily to encompass more.
Love is a well, a light, a star.

Keep stretching me, God, until my barriers become
so thin you can shine through me, like the sun.

22.

Clouds nest on the mountain's shoulders
like old friends stopping by for a chat.

The volcano is earth striving toward heaven,
creating fecund, new life.

Joy surges with a flare of sun
as light stitches together the divine and human.

23.

A foggy August morning, a chill
of autumn in the air.

The pomegranate tree by the wall holds its first
two tiny globes, one red, one gold.

Season after season drinking in light,
at last this life is bearing fruit.

24.

Late in August, the pomegranate puts forth
its first fruits. All June and July, buds have blossomed
and dropped off. When summer reaches its zenith,

its mirror image—winter—is most imminent.
Then the blossoms hold on and burgeon,
filling out with the sweet seeds of wisdom.

25.

The five points of the maple leaves
spread wide their clasp,
like fingers stretched to play octave chords.

Their red, gold, orange shimmers with sunlight,
beauty at its most intense
like piano notes struck, searing as they die away.

26.

Soup warming my stomach, Vivaldi swirling the air,
I surrender into satisfaction.
This life is indeed good.

Warmer yet, love's gold fire resting in the heart.
Sweeter yet, joy's music singing in the veins.
That full surrender opens into eternity.

27.

Connection is the essence of life:
as if we were not in separate bodies
but together make up one body.

For the life force within us flows between us
like electricity, like streams of life-giving blood,
feeding and guiding every single cell.

28.

Over a holiday meal our neighbor tells us
he'll again be pruning our pomegranate tree.

"It'll probably look like I killed it," he warns,
"but next year you'll have lots of pomegranates."

Wise in the ways of the harvest, he says,
"Only the new growth bears fruit."

29.

In wisdom is balance, harmony, moderation.
In wisdom is extravagance and delight.

In wisdom is surrender and trust.
In wisdom is peace and generosity.

Wisdom throws her golden cloak about us,
showering all in light and love.

30.

Tonight in the meditation circle, kneeling down,
closing my eyes, heat from burning candles hits my face,

scent of paraffin takes me home, where each heart opening
shares its light. This I can tell you with certainty:

find a door that opens into eternity,
go there often and knock.

Thirty Poems of Passion

1.

Diving in is the essential act.
Passion is immersion—in sound, light, flesh.

Pull the ripcord of your soul
and dare that soaring flight.

Life is a free-fall into death,
joyous abandon the flaring parachute.

2.

Hearing the majesty of Purcell's "Trumpet Voluntary"
at my mother's memorial, I imagine
gates of heaven opening to greet her.

And I wonder, was she trying to tell us
that the entire shape of life,
even its ending, can fill with beauty?

3.

On the flight back from Michigan,
I recall my mother's gifts to me:
music, dance, art, poetry, and thrift.

I was born last when she had mastered her craft,
immersing me in arts and travel.
Was guiding me perhaps her magnum opus?

4.

The passion of grief is like a river,
flowing from shock to acceptance.

Only by diving in
can we find our way downstream.

Perhaps grief teaches a joining together of opposites:
pain with joy, brokenness with gratitude.

5.

Where is the passion in grief?
Is it in the deep weeping, the loneliness,
feeling like a motherless child?

Could it also be in the passion of God
throwing her arms around us each
like a lost child she will never let go?

6.

Orange roses float among white orchids;
gardenias nest in branches, their perfume
filling the air like nightingale song.

My mother is gone from this Earth,
yet the beauty she loved—*ikebana*, Debussy—
sends out living vibrations, connecting us still.

7.

Walking down the red carpet, I see how small
the nominees really are. Then, from the balcony,
my vision telescopes, and the presenters look tiny.

This perception shifts my youngest child worldview,
where others look bigger, more competent, intimidating.
With new sight, I feel liberated to follow my bliss.

8.

The violet-speckled orchid sends out lush blooms
that last and last for months on end.

What fuels their persistence?
Is it depth of passion?

They are all root, filling the pot like a clenched fist,
ready to break through any barrier.

9.

This first spring day of sitting outdoors on the patio
uncaps the flow of passion, joy at being alive.

Like palm branches stretching out fingers to the light,
my soul expands, reaching out in all directions,

becomes transparent and buoyant as a soap bubble.
Now passion's dance is riotous new growth.

10.

What lies beneath this fear of earthquakes?
Death coming in the night to take me unawares?

A life unfinished that yet feels barely begun?
A shaking loose of what feels real and trusted?

Beloved, let your passion run like fire in my veins
to ignite with life all that I touch.

11.

Heat and languor pour down upon me.
The March sun rehearses its July fierceness.

The birds give voice to the running sap
as though all things could flow uphill.

Joy opens wide, a daffodil whose roots drink deep
of desire, passion, poetry—reviving life.

12.

Neither glowing skin, nor veins and muscles beneath,
slake thirst and desire in throat and heart.

The lover's touch, warm and comforting,
heralds the embrace of the Beloved

when all that is empty will be filled
and all that is filled will be emptied.

Then only will the Beloved stand
in burning truth, at one.

13.

The piano that thundered above her childish head
now stands in her home like a well-groomed mount
eager to be put through its paces.

Where is the door that opens to passion in music,
where sound swirls like exotic incense,
inflaming the soul for the touch of the deity?

14.

Grief's passion surges through lungs and fingertips;
you wail and beat the keyboard.

Pain becomes energy, becomes sound flowing out,
reverberating across space and time.

Where your mother sat and played for years, you now sit,
feeling her echo beside you, playing as in a duet.

And you imagine the power she felt commanding the keyboard,
shimmering the air with vibrating art.

15.

Let us recall the point of the passion stories—
Siddhartha holding firm amid swirling delusions,
daring to become a cup filled with Light.

Yeshua on the cross, groaning his labors
to birth more Light into the world.
In every struggle, look for the wound where Light bleeds in.

16.

At the heart of our meditation circle,
warmth and light flow out from a dozen candles.

Together in community, our hearts unite
and great warmth is born to beat back cold,
greater light is born to beat back night.

Friends, our circle is a golden raft,
carrying us through treacherous seas.

17.

It is hunger for God that lights the flame.
At first each poem is but a matchstick
held out against the darkness.

Put your breath into it. Once the Beloved's
breath is breathing you, the flame leaps
like a child inside and feeds on pure love.

18.

Take off the glasses of perceiving dualities
and see no separation between living and dying.
Anything else is a lie.

Trees shaking their palms and birds twittering
know it. Their joy is boundless, for always
and everywhere living interleaves with dying.

19.

Pink and yellow roses bloom again in my garden.
Do they know my mother is gone?
Do they know how excited she got just hearing of them?

In my dead heart—my heart that believes it has died as well—
let the roses come back to bloom, let me allow joy
to open its heavy yellow bud, its petals like wings in the sky.

20.

There was once a whale who thought to live
outside the sea, but laying there beached

felt the crushing pain of his own immensity
without the embrace of the one who created him that way.

The pain of separation is a game the mind plays,
seducing itself to believe one can live outside God.

It is as easy for the soul to live outside God
as for a whale to live outside the sea.

21.

The pomegranate tree puts forth its first two buds.
How is it the pain of grief transforms?
What falls away from us with the dead?

What do we hold closer, as we the living
carry forward our dead in our fragile hearts?
Where there is cutting, later come buds and blossoms.

22.

Passion's fire cleanses me.
Passion's wind fills my sails.

Let passion turn the key to free the prisoner
from a cell whose bars are fear.

Let passion's boat with billowing sails
ferry me over to the shore called love.

23.

Today I know that each person's death
leaves a gap as wide as the Grand Canyon.

All order, all sense, broken and shattered.
Emotional ties torn out like fingernails.

Into this cold, barren canyon, dear God,
send a wild, rushing stream of new life.

24.

Pain can be a purifier.
Dis-ease can teach us our true priorities.

Old defenses can slough off like dead skin,
false self peeling off like out-of-date clothes.

Let these wounds in us cleanse us,
shedding all that's not true Self, not God.

25.

The way to pull the plug on pain is forgiveness:
stagnant darkness swirls down the drain.

Forgiveness cleans the teeth of the soul, scrubs
behind its ears, scrapes blame from under its fingernails.

Wet as a butterfly fresh from the chrysalis,
the soul dries in the sun and takes flight.

26.

Sometimes it takes a breaking of our hard
shells to open us to passion.

Perhaps the pain we feel is just the
openness, so unfamiliar that it burns.

Perhaps what this rawness really needs
is a balm of healing love.

27.

When passion becomes compassion,
the burning pain within cools.

It is connectedness that soothes
the soul's fevered brow.

None of us is alone, because we are
always swimming in the Beloved, together.

28.

When that old invisible ghost starts shaking the table,
sit down on top like Siddhartha and ride out the whole storm.

Throw yourself on God's mercy, cling to
God's long braids, nestle against God's bosom.

In the place where strength and softness meet,
God's arms will ever enfold you.

29.

The buzzing saw next door cuts through my contemplation
as does the pain of grief and fear.

Yet the saw's job is just as much a part of the day
as the Cessna zooming overhead, the wind rustling
palm fronds, the sun warming my skin.

Let my contemplation encompass the saw,
encompassing all to encompass God.

30.

The nature of pain, just as the nature of grief,
is a belief in separateness.

When separateness finally falls away
like the husk of a seed drinking in sun,

like the clothing of lovers delighting in union,
the soul—stripped of illusion—bathes in God.

Thirty Poems of Peace

1.

What do you think peace is anyway?
Absence of worry, pain, strife?
Or fullness of divine love inflating you like a balloon?

Listen closely, when you're ready to experience peace,
open the valve at the crown of your head,

and the divine love that's been itching to get inside
will rush in, filling you completely,
pushing everything else out.

2.

Write all your worries in a letter to God
and mail it to the Divine with a song.

Detail every grievance life has laid upon you.
Dance it out so the Beloved knows every step.

Let grief and pain move out. When you are finally
empty, peace will move in and begin remodeling.

3.

Peace is not an only child. She is a middle child,
really the second-born of triplets.

Her big sister, Love, opens the way with surrender.
Peace follows behind, mirroring everything Love does.

Joy is the playful littlest sister, full of pranks to shake
things up and wanting more than anything to dance.

4.

Let me pour words into you like rain on parched earth.
What looks like a storm cloud coming on
is really heralding the Beloved's presence.

Love is everywhere. No one can help tripping over it
like a toddler's playfully scattered toys.
Open to the pouring of a great rain of peace.

5.

Dear ones, let go all your striving, let go
all desire to be something grand,
to build of your life a pyramid or palace.

Rather, carve into your soul a hollow place
and sand it smooth to create a bowl.
Dance in the rain to catch God
in your bowl and offer a drink to all.

6.

Standing still as a tree planted in the garden,
rooting energy deep in Mother Earth,
I am filled with calm and spaciousness.

My heart knows a wisdom to share with you:
only a deep well fills with blessed peace,
and the digging of it is all silence.

7.

A balloon filled with warm air from an ardent fire
soars and plays on the breeze,
traversing a great expanse of countryside.

Beloved, let the heat of my heart
fill my being with peace and spaciousness,
floating on joy through this eternal journey.

8.

Under a mostly clouded sky,
cooler after a record heat,
there is great gentleness in the softened light.

As though God were whispering
in a mother's tender voice:
Be at peace, dear ones; all is well.

9.

God calls us to find new lovers.
Your spirit needs a divorce from fear.

Fear is the spouse our parents picked out for us.
Now we are awake and it's our time to choose.

Let your spirit find a lover
who is playful and at peace.

Let the union of deep yearning
be for what's both present and beyond.

10.

God, split me wide like ripe fruit.
Like a pomegranate drunk on sunlight
busting open with jeweled seeds.

God, I am ripe for the picking.
Let the sweet and tart juice of my words
be a balm of wisdom and peace to those who hear.

11.

In this morning's rain the world grows silent
almost as if it were nighttime
and this yearning was for the golden sun of day.

This yearning is for the Beloved's radiant love
to blaze through me, for the breath of God
to fill this humble flute and let it sing.

12.

Ease now flows like honey, sweet and golden.
It is surrender to the Beloved's touch.

Let the Beloved's lips breathe into you.
Let the Beloved's arms support you.

Shed the old shell of dis-ease,
taste the sweet-honeyed flow of ease.

13.

Like an adoring dog awaiting your return,
the trees stand there wagging their palm fronds.

They are ready to slobber all over you
with shade and oxygen, meeting your essential needs.

God's trees watch over you like sheepdogs,
modeling the devotion that opens into peace.

14.

Why does the moon shine less brightly than the sun?
Is it because she thinks herself less?

Could it be that any thought of comparison dims our light?
The way of perfection is non-perfection: no shoulds or have-tos.

Peace flows in the experience of oneness with all.
Peace flows in a deep stream mingled with justice and love.

15.

In Zumba class we jump from side to side
and wave our arms above our heads.

Ecstasy unfolds in me like a giant white bird,
wings spanning my arms, lifting me to kiss joy's face.

I know no delight as great as this eternal dance:
when I am so empty of me and so full of God.

16.

A bit of motion caught from the corner of my eye:
my processing brain creates a spider crawling on the shelf.

It is the fear within our psyches
that we project on the unseen, the unknown.

When we empty the storehouse of negative images,
all that's left are peace, joy, and ease.

17.

What can I tell you about peace?
Is it an ever-flowing river, a stream?

Let all your practices be for building a fountain there.
Jump in the water and stand under its cool pounding.

And don't forget to splash others;
toss them in when they least expect it.

18.

We are each a piece of the peace.
We are each a cell in the body of God.

When we all fire together like muscle fiber,
our beating hearts a precision drill team,

then miracles can happen. We can build
pyramids of love and temples of joy.

19.

Life's precious dance is dancing in me.
Energy swirls through me like bursts of lightning.

Breath flies in and out like the monarchs migrating.
Cells dance in their salt tides like anemones feeding.

Bones meditate with great stillness in their marrow.
The Beloved is the dancer now becoming the dance.

20.

Peace is found in the stillness.
Look for it there by quieting the mind.

Let the traffic of your atoms slow.
Let the fist around your heart relax its grip

so your heart floats upward like a balloon—
yearning, disappearing, finally bursting to join God.

21.

The journey from pain to peace
flows like a river twisting between high banks.
There is no getting there without getting wet.

The traveler would do well
to dive in, go headfirst.
Let the water course down your cheeks.

22.

This Advent season I now comprehend:
we humans have not been waiting thousands of years
for Love to arrive just once.

Love arrives every year, every day, every second.
In each breath is the choice to let God
give birth, in and through us, to the sacred.

23.

Hunting for God is a skill the wise develop.
Sometimes we need to seduce the great Seducer.

Like blood on the waters to attract
a great beast that will consume us,

we spread our song, our art, as widely as we can
trusting we will soon be devoured by God.

24.

Ease is a golden balm that fills us if we let it.
Ease is like drinking in honey
through a blowhole in our heads.

Smoke out the bees of thoughts and emotions,
completely fill with sweet light—
all action becomes poetry and dance.

25.

Lean in closely and I will whisper to you:
there is a secret language to communicate with Love.
Poetry is the language of intimacy with God.

Come nearer yet. It is not I who call but the Beloved.
Lift your pen, brush, guitar, soul—for to create
is to let God dance within you.

26.

Sitting on the patio eating a pomegranate
as though in the hanging gardens of Baghdad,
I see how hard it is not to swallow a seed.

I think of Persephone and the nature of human life:
half in the underworld, half in the topside world,
half in grief, half in joy and peace.

27.

A grain of sand that thinks it's alone
on the beach will never be at peace.

Peace comes from knowing our true state.
We are always and everywhere connected to each other.

We are always and everywhere connected to God.
In life or death, we are always in God.

28.

The Beloved is the ground of all Being, and yet
the Beloved's being takes root in each creature and plant.

We are all rooted in each other—our leaves and branches,
arms and hands, form one great creation.

Peace flows from trust, and trust from knowledge:
our oneness is certain, unbroken, unbreakable.

29.

Peace is in the surrender,
the letting go, the softening.

Unclench the mind's fists. Wash the laundry
of old beliefs and hang it out to dry.

There in the warm sun where your spirit blows in the breeze,
there is found truth and deepest trust in the Friend.

30.

Remember, dear ones, peace is a choice.
Even amidst crashing waves of grief, pain, despair

stands a lighthouse with a glowing beacon,
warm as sunlight, pouring out love. Swim for it.

Even amid the cacophony of worry, frustration, anger
a clear true note shimmers. Tune your ears to peace.

ACKNOWLEDGMENTS

Let me begin at the beginning. I am only writing today by the grace of God. My parents, Joseph and Doris Datsko, gave their five children an upbringing enriched by the arts: music and dance lessons, arts and crafts, concerts, singing in church choir. In high school, my English teachers, Miss Reynolds and Dr. Swenson-Davis, challenged me to develop my writing. In college, I majored in creative writing, choreography, and psychology of creativity through the mentoring of Professors Walter Clark, Vera Embree, and Rudolf Arnheim. My Aunt Clara also encouraged me to embrace being a writer. And when I met my soulmate, Dr. José Sánchez-H., he became the greatest champion and co-conspirator of my creative endeavors. His are the first eyes to see each poem I write, and he patiently proofreads my work before it goes out into the world.

For the growth of my writing in the direction of spiritual poetry, I want to thank some of the gardeners whose care helped it flourish. The Reverend Mary Ellen Kilsby and the Reverend Libby Tigner celebrated my early attempts. The Reverend Jerald Stinson helped me to engage collaboratively with clergy. Cathy Chambers brainstormed with me on making an artist book, a project from which all of this poetry has flowed. Later, as Moderator at the First Congregational Church of Long Beach, Cathy was instrumental in my being awarded the Aaron and Maycie Herrington Pathfinder Award and being given the honorary title of Poet in Residence, both of which opened this "pathless path" before me.

The community of the First Congregational Church of Long Beach provided fertile ground in which my creative process grew deep roots. Thus rooted, poetry began to flow through me, both for liturgical use and for these volumes. The Sacred Practices meditation group, which I co-lead with Dr. Bob Kalayjian, has offered the cross-pollination of both hearing and sharing poems. I am grateful to Dr. Bob and all my fellow meditators. Gratitude also flows to others who have been part of the FCCLB community. Megan Monaghan shared with me a collection of poetry by Hafiz that scattered more seeds. Composer Stan DeWitt set seven of the poems as "Seven Songs of Longing." Additionally, Director of Music Curtis Heard set some of the poems for liturgical use. The Reverend John Forrest Douglas made a video of one of my poems.

I especially want to thank the godmothers and godfathers of these books. The Reverend Mary Scifres read *Swimming in God* and recommended I try The Pilgrim Press. The Reverend Elena Larssen spoke with and wrote a letter of introduction for me to The Pilgrim Press, as well as the foreword to *Dancing Through Fire*. The Reverend Molly Baskette wrote an endorsement for me to send to the publisher and also the foreword for *Singing Fierce Gratitude*. The Reverend Jim Burklo gave me many doses of encouragement and wrote the foreword for *Drinking Pure Light*. The Reverend Maren Tirabassi invited me to share my poetry on her blog and wrote the foreword for *Swimming in God*.

As publisher of The Pilgrim Press, the Reverend Rachel Hackenberg humbled me with her radical welcome of the four manuscripts. I am deeply grateful to her for believing in this poetry. Licensing coordinator Kathryn Martin has valiantly answered my many questions and helped me through the process. Program assistant Georgetta Thomas coordinated schedules and communications. Production coordinator Adam Bresnahan guided the manuscripts into book form. My gratitude to each of them as well.

My heartfelt thanks to my attorney Phillip Rosen for his thoughtful and generous support with the publishing agreements. Gratitude also to my friend Nancy Schraeder for her many years of encouragement and her careful proofreading. Many thanks as well to Suzanne Lyons, whose career coaching gave me the tools to implement my dreams.

ABOUT THE AUTHOR

Tina Datsko de Sánchez is an author and filmmaker whose work won fourteen Hopwood Awards and the Los Angeles Arts Council Award. Her writing appeared in magazines and books in several countries, including *Michigan Magazine, Nimrod, Psychological Perspectives, Sojourners* and *The Heroine's Journey Workbook.* Her bilingual poetry book, *The Delirium of Simón Bolívar,* published jointly by Floricanto Press and Berkeley Press with a foreword by Edward James Olmos, won the Phi Kappa Phi Award and a Michigan Council for the Arts Grant. She wrote and produced the feature documentary *Searching for Simón Bolívar: One Poet's Journey*, which premiered at the 30th Festival of Latin American Cinema in Trieste, Italy. Her poetry films aired on Sundance Channel and CNN Showbiz Today. She taught creative writing at The University of Michigan and screenwriting at California State University, Long Beach. She serves as Poet in Residence at the First Congregational Church in Long Beach, where she resides.

WORKS BY TINA DATSKO DE SÁNCHEZ

POETRY

Singing Fierce Gratitude

Drinking Pure Light

Swimming in God

The Delirium of Simón Bolívar (translated by José Sánchez-H.)

FILMS (as Writer/Producer)

Searching for Simón Bolívar: One Poet's Journey

The Candle

Crossing the Andes

Robinson

Domitila Speaks to the Earth

The Pomegranate

The Millstone

My General

The Man of Laws

The Delirium

News for Manuela

The Road to the Coast

Rudolf Arnheim: A Life in Art

La Paz (co-written with José Sánchez-H.)

Yo no entiendo a la gente grande

PLAYS

Manuelita

La Paz (co-authored with José Sánchez-H.)